A Handy

Journal

for

Science Fiction

Writers

Book

&

Author

Information

Record your author information, book's title, ISBN numbers, ASIN number and Publication date.

Book Information

Title: _____

Author: _____

Publisher: _____

ASIN (Amazon eBook) _____

ISBN: 10-_____ ISBN: 13-_____

If you have published your eBook on Smashwords or another site that requires a different ISBN Number, record below

ISBN: 10-_____ ISBN: 13-_____

Number of pages: _____ Genre: _____

Keywords: _____

_____

Publishing Sites

Amazon Paperback	☐	Amazon eBook	☐
Goodreads	☐	Smashwords	☐
Barnes & Noble Paperback	☐	Barnes & Noble eBook	☐
iBook	☐	Kobo	☐
Other _____	☐	Other _____	☐
Other _____	☐	Other _____	☐

Pre-Release Date: _____

Release Date: _____

Book Descriptions:

Hook: (A sentence to" hook" the reader to want more. Example: She was never meant to be born human.) _____

_____

_____

Short Description: File Name & Place _____

Description:_____

_____

_____

_____

Long Description: File name & Place _____

Description: _____

_____

_____

_____

_____

_____

_____

_____

_____

_____

_____

_____

_____

_____

_____

_____

_____

_____

_____

Author Information

Author name _____

Author Short Bio: _____

_____

_____

_____

_____

_____

_____

_____

_____

_____

_____

Author Long Bio: File name & Place _____

Description: _____

_____

_____

_____

_____

_____

_____

_____

_____

_____

_____

_____

_____

_____

_____

_____

_____

_____

_____

Characters

And their characteristics

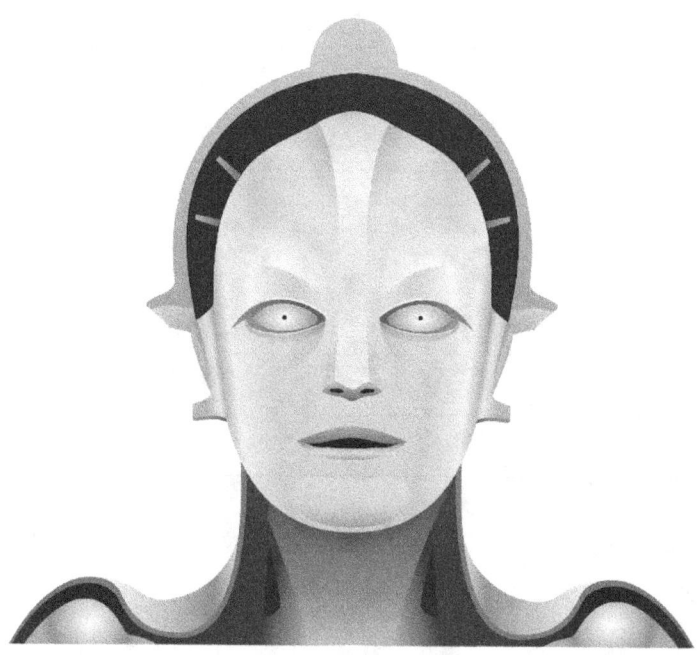

Record the names of your main and secondary characters, their hair, eye and skin color, height, unique characteristics and a description.

Record the names and a brief description of minor characters.

Main Character #1 - Name: _____

From planet _____

Hair color: _____ Eye Color: _____

Skin Color: _____ Height: _____

Unique Characteristic: _____

Description: _____

_____

_____

_____

_____

Main Character #2 - Name: _____

From planet: _____

Hair color: _____ Eye Color: _____

Skin Color: _____ Height: _____

Unique Characteristic: _____

Description: _____

_____

_____

_____

Main Character #3 - Name: _____

From planet _____

Hair color: _____ Eye Color: _____

Skin Color: _____ Height: _____

Unique Characteristic: _____

Description: _____

_____

_____

_____

_____

Main Character #4 - Name: _____

From planet: _____

Hair color: _____ Eye Color: _____

Skin Color: _____ Height: _____

Unique Characteristic: _____

Description: _____

_____

_____

_____

Character #1 - Name: _____

From planet _____

Hair color: _____ Eye Color: _____

Skin Color: _____ Height: _____

Unique Characteristic: _____

Description: _____

_____

_____

_____

_____

Character #2 - Name: _____

From planet: _____

Hair color: _____ Eye Color: _____

Skin Color: _____ Height: _____

Unique Characteristic: _____

Description: _____

_____

_____

_____

Character #3 - Name: _____

From planet _____

Hair color: _____ Eye Color: _____

Skin Color: _____ Height: _____

Unique Characteristic: _____

Description: _____

_____

_____

_____

_____

Character #4 - Name: _____

From planet: _____

Hair color: _____ Eye Color: _____

Skin Color: _____ Height: _____

Unique Characteristic: _____

Description: _____

_____

_____

_____

Character #5 - Name: _____

From planet _____

Hair color: _____ Eye Color: _____

Skin Color: _____ Height: _____

Unique Characteristic: _____

Description: _____

_____

_____

_____

_____

Character #6 - Name: _____

From planet: _____

Hair color: _____ Eye Color: _____

Skin Color: _____ Height: _____

Unique Characteristic: _____

Description: _____

_____

_____

_____

Character #7 - Name: _____

From planet _____

Hair color: _____ Eye Color: _____

Skin Color: _____ Height: _____

Unique Characteristic: _____

Description: _____

_____

_____

_____

_____

Character #8 - Name: _____

From planet: _____

Hair color: _____ Eye Color: _____

Skin Color: _____ Height: _____

Unique Characteristic: _____

Description: _____

_____

_____

_____

Minor Characters

Name: _____ Description: _____

_____

_____

Name: _____ Description: _____

_____

_____

Name: _____ Description: _____

_____

_____

Name: _____ Description: _____

_____

_____

Name: _____ Description: _____

_____

_____

Name: _____ Description: _____

_____

_____

Name: _____ Description: _____

_____

_____

Name: _____ Description: _____

_____

_____

Name: _____ Description: _____

_____

_____

Name: _____ Description: _____

_____

_____

Name: _____ Description: _____

_____

_____

Worlds

and

Places

Record the name of your main world, its location and description

Record other worlds of importance

Record minor worlds that are referenced

Main World's Name: _____

Location: _____

Description: _____

_____

_____

_____

_____

Beings that live there: _____

_____

Importance to Story: _____

_____

#2 World's Name: _____

Location: _____

Description: _____

_____

_____

_____

_____

Beings that live there: _____

_____

Importance to Story: _____

_____

#3 World's Name: _____

Location: _____

Description: _____

_____

_____

_____

_____

Beings that live there: _____

_____

Importance to Story: _____

_____

#4 World's Name: _____

Location: _____

Description: _____

_____

_____

_____

_____

Beings that live there: _____

_____

Importance to Story: _____

_____

#5 World's Name: _____

Location: _____

Description: _____

_____

_____

_____

_____

Beings that live there: _____

_____

Importance to Story: _____

_____

#6 World's Name: _____

Location: _____

Description: _____

_____

_____

_____

_____

Beings that live there: _____

_____

Importance to Story: _____

_____

Other Places of Importance

Place: _____

Importance: _____

Location: _____

Notes: _____

Place: _____

Importance: _____

Location: _____

Notes: _____

Place: _____

Importance: _____

Location: _____

Notes: _____

Place: _____

Importance: _____

Location: _____

Notes: _____

Plots

and

Subplots

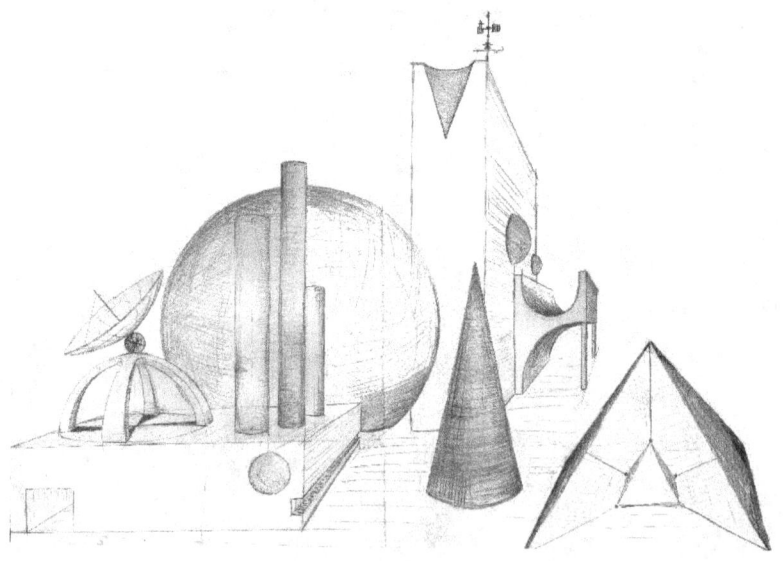

Record the main plot of your story and indicate important key components.

Record any subplots such as conflicts, hatreds, loves, relationships

Main Plot

Brief description of story: _____

_____

_____

_____

_____

_____

Important Points Not to Forget

#1 _____

#2 _____

#3 _____

#4 _____

#5 _____

#6 _____

Relationships

#1 _____

#2 _____

#3 _____

#4 _____

#5 _____

Conflicts

#1 _____

#2 _____

#3 _____

#4 _____

#5 _____

Notes

_____

_____

_____

_____

_____

_____

_____

_____

_____

_____

_____

_____

_____

Subplots

Subplot #1 Premises: _____

_____

_____

Characters Involved: _____

_____

Outcome: _____

_____

Resolved: Yes : _____   No_____

    Will be resolved at later date _____   When _____

_____

Subplot #2 Premises: _____

_____

_____

Characters Involved: _____

_____

Outcome: _____

_____

Resolved: Yes : _____   No_____

    Will be resolved at later date _____   When _____

_____

Subplot #3 Premises: _____

_____

_____

Characters Involved: _____

_____

Outcome: _____

_____

Resolved: Yes : _____   No_____

    Will be resolved at later date _____   When _____

_____

Issues needing to be addressed

Issue #1: _____

_____

Chapter or Page: _____

Actions needed: _____

_____

Issue #2: _____

_____

Actions needed: _____

_____

Chapter or Page _____

Issue #4: _____

_____

Chapter or Page: _____

Actions needed: _____

_____

Issue #5: _____

_____

Chapter or Page _____

Actions needed: _____

_____

Issue #6: _____

_____

Chapter or Page: _____

Actions needed: _____

_____

Issue #7: _____

_____

Chapter or Page: _____

Actions needed: _____

_____

Issue #8: _____

_____

Chapter or Page: _____

Actions needed: _____

_____

Notes

_____

_____

_____

_____

_____

_____

_____

_____

_____

_____

_____

_____

_____

_____

_____

Chapter

Outline

Record the title and synopsis of each chapter. Also the characters involved and any actions carried over into the next chapter or further into the book.

Chapter 1 Title: _____

What happens: _____

_____

_____

Characters involved: _____

_____

Story line carried forward: _____

_____

_____

Note: _____

_____

_____

Chapter 2 Title: _____

What happens: _____

_____

Characters involved: _____

_____

Story line carried forward: _____

_____

_____

Note: _____

_____

_____

Chapter 3 Title: _____

What happens: _____

_____

Characters involved: _____

_____

Story line carried forward: _____

_____

_____

Note: _____

_____

_____

Chapter 4 Title: _____

What happens: _____

_____

Characters involved: _____

_____

Story line carried forward: _____

_____

_____

Note: _____

_____

_____

Chapter 5 Title: _____

What happens: _____

_____

Characters involved: _____

_____

Story line carried forward: _____

_____

_____

Note: _____

_____

_____

Chapter 6 Title: _____

What happens: _____

_____

Characters involved: _____

_____

Story line carried forward: _____

_____

_____

Note: _____

_____

_____

Chapter 7 Title: _____

What happens: _____

_____

Characters involved: _____

_____

Story line carried forward: _____

_____

_____

Note: _____

_____

_____

Chapter 8 Title: _____

What happens: _____

_____

Characters involved: _____

_____

Story line carried forward: _____

_____

_____

Note: _____

_____

_____

Chapter 9 Title: _____

What happens: _____

_____

Characters involved: _____

_____

Story line carried forward: _____

_____

_____

Note: _____

_____

_____

Chapter 10 Title: _____

What happens: _____

_____

Characters involved: _____

_____

Story line carried forward: _____

_____

_____

Note: _____

_____

_____

Chapter 11 Title: _____

What happens: _____

_____

Characters involved: _____

_____

Story line carried forward: _____

_____

_____

Note: _____

_____

_____

Chapter 12 Title: _____

What happens: _____

_____

Characters involved: _____

_____

Story line carried forward: _____

_____

_____

Note: _____

_____

_____

Chapter 13 Title: _____

What happens: _____

_____

Characters involved: _____

_____

Story line carried forward: _____

_____

_____

Note: _____

_____

_____

Chapter 14 Title: _____

What happens: _____

_____

Characters involved: _____

_____

Story line carried forward: _____

_____

_____

Note: _____

_____

_____

Chapter 15 Title: _____

What happens: _____

_____

Characters involved: _____

_____

Story line carried forward: _____

_____

_____

Note: _____

_____

_____

Chapter 16 Title: _____

What happens: _____

_____

Characters involved: _____

_____

Story line carried forward: _____

_____

_____

Note: _____

_____

_____

Chapter 17 Title: _____

What happens: _____

_____

Characters involved: _____

_____

Story line carried forward: _____

_____

_____

Note: _____

_____

_____

Chapter 18 Title: _____

What happens: _____

_____

Characters involved: _____

_____

Story line carried forward: _____

_____

_____

Note: _____

_____

_____

Chapter 19 Title: _____

What happens: _____

_____

Characters involved: _____

_____

Story line carried forward: _____

_____

_____

Note: _____

_____

_____

Chapter 20 Title: _____

What happens: _____

_____

Characters involved: _____

_____

Story line carried forward: _____

_____

_____

Note: _____

_____

_____

Chapter 21 Title: _____

What happens: _____

_____

Characters involved: _____

_____

Story line carried forward: _____

_____

_____

Note: _____

_____

_____

Chapter 22 Title: _____

What happens: _____

_____

Characters involved: _____

_____

Story line carried forward: _____

_____

_____

Note: _____

_____

_____

Chapter 23 Title: _____

What happens: _____

_____

Characters involved: _____

_____

Story line carried forward: _____

_____

_____

Note: _____

_____

_____

Chapter 24 Title: _____

What happens: _____

_____

Characters involved: _____

_____

Story line carried forward: _____

_____

_____

Note: _____

_____

_____

Chapter 25 Title: _____

What happens: _____

_____

Characters involved: _____

_____

Story line carried forward: _____

_____

_____

Note: _____

_____

_____

Chapter 26 Title: _____

What happens: _____

_____

Characters involved: _____

_____

Story line carried forward: _____

_____

_____

Note: _____

_____

_____

Chapter 27 Title: _____

What happens: _____

_____

Characters involved: _____

_____

Story line carried forward: _____

_____

_____

Note: _____

_____

_____

Chapter 28 Title: _____

What happens: _____

_____

Characters involved: _____

_____

Story line carried forward: _____

_____

_____

Note: _____

_____

_____

Chapter 29 Title: _____

What happens: _____

_____

Characters involved: _____

_____

Story line carried forward: _____

_____

_____

Note: _____

_____

_____

Chapter 30 Title: _____

What happens: _____

_____

Characters involved: _____

_____

Story line carried forward: _____

_____

_____

Note: _____

_____

_____

Chapter 31 Title: _____

What happens: _____

_____

Characters involved: _____

_____

Story line carried forward: _____

_____

_____

Note: _____

_____

_____

Chapter 32 Title: _____

What happens: _____

_____

Characters involved: _____

_____

Story line carried forward: _____

_____

_____

Note: _____

_____

_____

Chapter 33 Title: _____

What happens: _____

_____

Characters involved: _____

_____

Story line carried forward: _____

_____

_____

Note: _____

_____

_____

Chapter 34 Title: _____

What happens: _____

_____

Characters involved: _____

_____

Story line carried forward: _____

_____

_____

Note: _____

_____

_____

Chapter 35 Title: _____

What happens: _____

_____

Characters involved: _____

_____

Story line carried forward: _____

_____

_____

Note: _____

_____

_____

Chapter 36 Title: _____

What happens: _____

_____

Characters involved: _____

_____

Story line carried forward: _____

_____

_____

Note: _____

_____

_____

Chapter 37 Title: _____

What happens: _____

_____

Characters involved: _____

_____

Story line carried forward: _____

_____

_____

Note: _____

_____

_____

Chapter 38 Title: _____

What happens: _____

_____

Characters involved: _____

_____

Story line carried forward: _____

_____

_____

Note: _____

_____

_____

Chapter 39 Title: _____

What happens: _____

_____

Characters involved: _____

_____

Story line carried forward: _____

_____

_____

Note: _____

_____

_____

Chapter 40 Title: _____

What happens: _____

_____

Characters involved: _____

_____

Story line carried forward: _____

_____

_____

Note: _____

_____

_____

Chapter 41 Title: _____

What happens: _____

_____

Characters involved: _____

_____

Story line carried forward: _____

_____

_____

Note: _____

_____

_____

Chapter 42 Title: _____

What happens: _____

_____

Characters involved: _____

_____

Story line carried forward: _____

_____

_____

Note: _____

_____

_____

Chapter 43 Title: _____

What happens: _____

_____

Characters involved: _____

_____

Story line carried forward: _____

_____

_____

Note: _____

_____

_____

Chapter 44 Title: _____

What happens: _____

_____

Characters involved: _____

_____

Story line carried forward: _____

_____

_____

Note: _____

_____

_____

Chapter 45 Title: _____

What happens: _____

_____

Characters involved: _____

_____

Story line carried forward: _____

_____

_____

Note: _____

_____

_____

Chapter 46 Title: _____

What happens: _____

_____

Characters involved: _____

_____

Story line carried forward: _____

_____

_____

Note: _____

_____

_____

Chapter 47 Title: _____

What happens: _____

_____

Characters involved: _____

_____

Story line carried forward: _____

_____

_____

Note: _____

_____

_____

Chapter 48 Title: _____

What happens: _____

_____

Characters involved: _____

_____

Story line carried forward: _____

_____

_____

Note: _____

_____

_____

Chapter 49 Title: _____

What happens: _____

_____

Characters involved: _____

_____

Story line carried forward: _____

_____

_____

Note: _____

_____

_____

Chapter 50 Title: _____

What happens: _____

_____

Characters involved: _____

_____

Story line carried forward: _____

_____

_____

Note: _____

_____

_____

Alien

Words

(As you invent alien words, record them with their meaning.)

Word	Definition

Word	Definition

Word	Definition

Word	Definition

Word	Definition

Other
Important
Stuff

Author's Website

Website address: http://www. _____

Date published: _____

Website Builder: _____

Number of Pages: _____

Website E-mail address: _____

What is included: _____

_____

_____

_____

_____

_____

_____

_____

Copyright

Date copyright applied for_____

File Number: _____

Date certificate received: _____

Notes

For information on the EUROPA Saga,

go to http://www.prgarcia1.com

The Europa Saga

A tale of suspense, adventure, assassins, survival and truth. Start the adventure today.

Get book one, EUROPA Awakenings, for free at
https://www.smashwords.com/books/view/633078

Additional available journals by P. R. Garcia

Address Books

Journals

Writing help

For sale on Amazon

or

Click on the JOURNAL page at http://www.prgarcia1.com

www.ingramcontent.com/pod-product-compliance
Lightning Source LLC
Chambersburg PA
CBHW060218290526
45789CB00003B/1320